# No Ordinary Child

L.G.C.M.
OXFORD HOUSE
DERBYSHIRE STREET
LONDON, E2 6HG, UK

# No Ordinary Child

*A Christian mother's acceptance
of her gay son*

Jacqueline Ley

WILD GOOSE PUBLICATIONS

First published 2002 by
Wild Goose Publications
Fourth Floor, Savoy House, 140 Sauchiehall Street,
Glasgow G2 3DH, UK
Wild Goose Publications is the publishing division of the Iona Community.
Scottish Charity No. SCO03794. Limited Company Reg. No. SCO96243.

ISBN 1 901557 61 8

Cover design © 2001 Wild Goose Publications

A catalogue record for this book is available from the British Library.

Distributed in Australia by Willow Connection Pty Ltd, Unit 4A, 3-9 Kenneth
Road, Manly Vale, NSW 2093, Australia and in New Zealand by Pleroma,
Higginson Street, Otane 4170, Central Hawkes Bay, New Zealand.

Permission to reproduce any part of this work in Australia
or New Zealand should be sought from Willow Connection.

Printed by Bell & Bain, Thornliebank, Glasgow

# Contents

# Foreword by James Ley

There is no time of year 'as camp as Christmas'; there is also no time of year worse for 'coming out' to one's family. Boxing day is probably the biggest window of opportunity, but isn't it depressing enough? For this reason and a few others, I chose the October week holiday. A week I'd never really appreciated or understood suddenly became a lifeline. I felt optimistic that if I handled this well, by Christmas my sexuality would be accepted and we could enjoy playful family innuendo about fairy lights.

Telling my parents wasn't a courteous measure to prevent their finding out another way. I was in desperate need of their Christian and spiritual support. I was living in Manchester, having moved there after drama school in

Glasgow. I hadn't left behind a bohemian, self-indulgent, arty period of my life as you might expect. In fact I was recovering from an overdose of Christian fundamentalism and self-denial. My months in Manchester, combined with the support of an inclusive, gay-friendly church, MCC, had started me on the journey to find my true identity as a gay Christian.

Ironically, taking home my sexuality was far easier than taking home the 'Toronto blessing', as I'd tried years previously. My parents were no strangers to extremist Christianity. Early in their married life they had been part of a very disciplined Christian group. Mum had learned then the morally correct way of folding her underwear in her chest of drawers, something she still refuses to share with me despite my persistent interest. Mum and Dad were concerned about the effects this kind of dogmatic church was having on me. Little did they know just how damaging it was. Behind the mask of liberation and joy was confusion and pain. Towards the end of my time there I spoke to one of the senior pastors about my sexuality. Needless to say this was a very brave step for me.

He prayed for me, lent me a book and then never spoke to me about it again. Over a short period I made my excuses and left. I left the church, Glasgow and self-denial behind. Dramatic – even for an aspiring actor!

In Manchester, after taking an initial break from the church, but not God, I got my head together. Being a hundred per cent convinced I was gay and 83 per cent sure that God was OK with that, I decided to tell my parents both of the above things. The only preparation I'd given my mother was asking her for a 'Delia Smith cookery book' for Christmas. I wasn't scared about telling my parents, who are both loving, reasonable and supportive. However, I knew that they were very conscientious and thorough people and would have a journey to go on before we could play happy, gay families.

I'd been home for a day already and Mum had done a respectable amount of my laundry. (My father happened to be away on a business trip at the time.) We'd just had breakfast and I felt the urge to tell her. We were standing at opposite sides of the kitchen and I told her I was gay. Knowing that my mother reserves dramatic displays of emotion for more trivial things, I could tell from her subtle expression that she was really shocked and didn't know what to say. I felt her love and she was very supportive, although reserved, but I also realised she needed time to come to terms with this in her own way. I could give her the gay Christian literature and Bible references but I couldn't make sense of it all for her. Having no children myself, I couldn't understand how she felt. Coming out to her was the end of a long period of self-discovery for me but only the beginning of a similar journey for her.

James Ley

# Introduction

Eighteen months ago, my 23-year-old son James plucked up the courage to tell me he was gay. In common with many parents in a similar situation, my initial reaction was one of shock and deep pain. To me, at that time, it felt like bereavement – the death, as I saw it, of so many hopes and dreams for my son, of every mother's hope of a 'normal' life for their child.

The fact that I am a Christian, that James too is a committed Christian, only served to compound my anguish. The fundamentalist Christian tradition had ingrained in me the tainted conviction that homosexuality was somehow sin; that, whatever his relationship with God, my son had placed himself beyond the pale.

One of the things I have had to learn over the past

eighteen months is that 'beyond the pale' is where we find Christ in the deepest and most compassionate sense; that God incarnate chose to suffer *outside* a city wall; that what we crave for our children often has far more to do with some graven image of supposed 'normality' than with what God himself plans and approves for their lives.

This book doesn't make any claims to come up with definitive answers or establish doctrines of right and wrong. Far from it. One of the shackles I have had to try and shed in the course of the past few months is the pernicious fundamentalist tendency to sit in judgement of others.

I would also hate to give the impression that what I have written represents the resolution of all my own fears and perplexities. Rather, my aim is to share my initial faltering steps on a journey, one that I would not have chosen to take, but that God, in his love and wisdom, deemed necessary.

When James first talked to me about his homosexuality, I remember urging him not to shut God out of the situation. It was as much a plea to myself at the time as an attempt to encourage him. Since then we have had to suffer an insensitive 'Keep the Clause' campaign, asserting the need to retain an Act of Parliament which forbids teachers to address homosexual issues in schools. This was largely mounted under the banner of the Christian church, reinforcing the idea that God is in the business of shutting people out, that – inexplicably – gay Christians are brutally exempt from their Creator's unconditional love.

According to the campaigners, the sanctity of some largely fictitious 'ideal' family is under threat. In response, I would like to join with every parent of a beloved gay child and celebrate what families are really about – not some tidy, comfortable norm but the gloriously complicated collection of diverse individuals that the Almighty has created.

'No ordinary child.' When I came across the phrase one day in my Bible reading in Hebrews (Heb.11:23 NIV), it was as though God had lifted me up to see, with his eyes, not a freak, as James laughingly refers to himself at times, but a blessedly extraordinary person.

I realise in writing this series of meditations that, for many who do not subscribe to Christian belief, the inner struggles and tensions that I describe may seem alien or irrelevant. But although, for this reason, I'm writing primarily for Christian parents, I hope that 'the comfort with which I myself have been comforted of God' (2 Corinthians 1:4 AV) might be of use to any parent in similar circumstances, wherever they are on the spiritual journey.

In short, I pray that the collection of meditations in this book will lead other parents to give heartfelt thanks for the extraordinary.

# One

# The Journey to Solid Ground

In the early days of my struggle to come to terms with James's homosexuality, I identified very much with the experience that God describes in Isaiah 54:11 (AV), 'O thou afflicted, tossed with tempest and not comforted ...' At first, I couldn't see anything beyond the tempests of doubting and resenting God, agonising over the past and mistakes I might have made in James's upbringing, and storms of fear about his future and what life might hold for him.

But hard on the heels of my 'tempest' verse came a series of beautiful promises from God, including one that held special resonance. 'All your sons will be taught by the Lord, and great will be your children's peace.' (Isaiah 54:13 NIV)

Together, my husband and I have had the privilege

of bringing up three sons, two of them heterosexual and one of them gay, but this Isaiah promise made no distinction. God had undertaken to teach each one of them and to impart his peace to each of them in the process.

That 'all' was a timely introduction to an important aspect of my own journey to peace – that nothing could threaten the security and permanence of James's relationship with God; that the revelation of his homosexuality might have hit me like a thunderbolt but it certainly hadn't come as any surprise to his Creator.

## Step one

# 'Fearfully and wonderfully made'

*For thou hast possessed my inward parts; thou hast covered me in my mother's womb. I will praise thee; for I am fearfully and wonderfully made ... My substance was not hidden from thee, when I was made in secret, and intricately wrought in the lowest parts of the earth. Thine eyes did see my substance, yet being unformed; and in thy book, all my members were written, which in continuance were fashioned, when as yet there was none of them.* (Psalm 139:13–16 AV)

One of my greatest heartaches is that my son had to endure what many other gay youngsters continue to endure: the lonely anguish of hiding the very 'substance' of their personality from those around them, from family, from school friends, from teachers, even at times from themselves. But this substance is never hidden from God and, far from being something shameful, these verses say that the personality's substance is part of the beautiful intricacy and complexity of his creation.

A few months ago, I took part in an Ignation Retreat in Daily Life. The Ignation Sister who counselled me during that time posed many challenges to my preconceived ideas and one that has really stuck with me was the question of whether, given the necessary magic wand, I would choose to change James.

My initial glib reaction was 'Yes, I would wave my wand and make him heterosexual.'

But then I became aware of the danger in that kind of thinking. I could see that it was a little akin to wandering around the Tate Gallery or the Louvre with a paintbrush adjusting various masterpieces with a few haphazard blobs of paint. Given the chance to 'fix' my son's sexuality, what havoc might I wreak with the whole person, with his refreshingly divergent mind, his creative talents, his zany sense of humour, his remarkable ability to empathise with the feelings of others?

As I pondered this, I was reminded of verses from another Psalm, Ps. 80:15–19 in the Living Bible, 'Protect what you yourself have planted, the son you have raised for yourself ... strengthen the man you love, the son of your choice.'

Just as James is the son of God's choice, one whom he pledges to protect and nurture, I realised that he is also the son of my choice – exactly the kind of son in fact that, given the dubious benefit of a magic wand, I would have wished for with all my heart.

**Step two**

# 'In whom I am well pleased'

Step two was bound up with the first and taking it restored my pleasure in family photographs!

Like many families, our home is dotted with a year-by-year chronicle of family history: baby snaps, school photos, graduation pictures. This chronicle had become even more precious once our children had flown the nest, but in the aftermath of the breaking of James's 'news', I found to my shame and distress that I wanted to lock many of these photos away in a drawer, as though the smiling face of my middle son was one that I no longer recognised.

Then, one day, 2 Peter 1:17 (AV) took on new meaning for me. 'This is my beloved Son, in whom I am well pleased.'

'Why have you stopped being well pleased with *your* beloved son?' God seemed to be saying and he reminded me of verses that have always been among my 'favourites': Ephesians 1:4–5 (AV). 'According as He hath chosen us in Him before the foundation of the world, that we should be holy and without blame before him in love. Having predestinated us unto the adoption of sons by Jesus Christ to Himself, according to the good pleasure of His will, to the praise of the glory of His grace, through which He hath made us accepted in the Beloved.'

'Acceptance in the beloved', God was reminding me, is a universal status which excludes no one. It places all of us on a level playing-field where the only prerogative for anyone's child to be accepted is relationship with *God's* beloved child, Jesus Christ.

The fascist wing of the Christian Church, where

acceptance seems to be an alien concept, would try to assert that God has other prerogatives, but Ephesians 1 maintains otherwise. In my living-room that day, surrounded by family photographs, I relaxed in the fact that I may look at *all* my sons with pleasure, as God looks at them, 'accepted in the beloved'.

## Step three

# 'For there is no difference'

A prayer letter prompted the next step. Arriving through the post one day from missionary friends we had known years back, I found its contents inspired depression rather than the uplifting desire to pray. Their boys – all similar ages to ours – were, according to the letter, model Christian youngsters, engaged in every wholesome activity under the sun and requiring prayer only for a little fine tuning of their exemplary walks with God.

How different my own family 'story' seemed to be at the time, but God homed in on that word 'difference' as, later on that day, I turned to Romans 3:22–27 (AV). 'Even the righteousness of God which is by faith of Jesus Christ unto all and upon all them that believe; for there is no difference. For all have sinned and come short of the glory of God ... where is boasting then?'

God had to remind me again of a fundamental fact that underpins the whole of the Christian message: that God doesn't differentiate. As far as he is concerned, none of us have made it. Faith in Christ alone makes the crucial difference.

Perhaps that letter caught me at the wrong time, but it seems to me that prayer letters can turn prayer requests into boasting, a completely worldly exercise in spiritual one-upmanship. And I confess I have been guilty of the same kind of thing with one of those Christmas card family update newsletters, cataloguing the spectacular successes of every single family member, right down to the cat and the budgie!

A friend and colleague of ours, father of a large family of children and step-children, makes no bones about referring proudly to his 'gay son'. I'm not sure that I want to emulate this, mainly because I'm not in the habit of referring to my eldest and youngest offspring as my heterosexual sons, so see no reason why I should make an exception with the middle son who happens to be gay ... but I admire our friend's attitude. Like so many parents – and, sadly, Christian parents seem to be particularly guilty – I'm not very good at 'telling it like it is' about my children.

## Step four

# 'He who hath begun'

As a mother, I realise that over the years I have been used to planning and organising my children's lives. There's nothing wrong with this – it's part of being a responsible parent. But, if we are wise, we work towards gradually relinquishing that control. We accept that we are no longer responsible for teaching our children how they should live; that the decisions they make about their lives become their own responsibility.

I thought I had managed to take all this on board, but when James confided in me about his homosexuality I felt an immediate obligation to come up with some moral and spiritual pronouncements on the subject, some watertight formula about how he should live his life. 'Mother knows best' – or ought to – was my instant, reflex reaction and I expended quite a lot of nervous energy, fretting about what was the correct 'advice' to give my son.

Then God applied Isaiah 30:15 (AV) one day, as a gentle antidote to my fretfulness. 'In quietness and confidence shall be your strength.' 'That's all very well, God,' I felt like saying, 'but confidence in what?' God's answer came back swiftly in the shape of Philippians 1:6 (AV) – 'being confident of this very thing, that He which hath begun a good work in you (him) shall complete it until the day of Jesus Christ.'

As I pondered this verse, I felt great release and, at last, a real 'quietness'. It was God's responsibility, not mine, to show my son the right path. God had shouldered the task of completing what he'd begun, and James's homosexuality didn't exempt him in some way from his Creator's ongoing redemptive work in his life. I could have a part in this, I realised, through my prayerful, loving support, but it was 'the author and finisher of our faith' (Hebrews 12:2 AV) who bore the responsibility.

At the time when I came across the Hebrews verse, I had just completed the arduous, laborious process of writing a novel. I knew the dogged tenacity that was involved in following such a project through to the end – the false starts, the fresh beginnings, the weary temptation to give up at times, the need to keep re-focusing on the vision – and I drew tremendous encouragement from the fact that God was the author who would never give up, who had committed himself to seeing his masterpiece through to completion.

## Step five

# 'And fled from them naked'

From time to time, a particular Bible verse or passage moves me to tears, and Mark 14:51–52 (AV) did that for me recently. Judas has just betrayed Jesus in the Garden of Gethsemane. His other disciples have deserted him and fled but we are told: 'There followed him a certain young man, having a linen cloth cast about his naked body. And the young men laid hold on him; and he left the linen cloth, and fled from them naked.'

There was something about the description of this young man that caught me on the raw, with its poignant picture of nakedness and vulnerability, coupled with the urgent, desperate desire to be with Jesus. We don't know who he was; his name isn't recorded in the Gospels and his need to be with his Lord was thwarted by a gang of young thugs who dragged him away, exposing and mocking him in the process.

As I read over those verses, the unknown young man seemed to personify painfully for me the plight of so many homosexuals, hounded away from Christ by the bigoted thuggery of some Christians, and I could hardly bear to keep reading.

But the God of all comfort brought me back to the psalm that began this chapter, Psalm 139: 'O Lord thou hast searched him and known him.'

'Who the young man was who followed Jesus is not known,' my Bible Commentary states simply of Mark 14:51, but Jesus knew who he was, and he alone was the shield to the young man's vulnerability and the answer to his need.

Two

# The Journey to Surrendered Responsibility

Recently, I attended a meeting of my church house group where the discussion turned to bringing up children. One older lady in the group, a mother and grandmother, volunteered the opinion that the only real way to experience peace about adult children was to 'let go' of them.

Her quiet wisdom struck a chord with me. It fitted with what I'd been thinking recently about allowing God to bear the responsibility. 'Letting go' here wasn't a case of 'giving up on' but rather of 'handing over', of allowing God free rein to do all that was needful, in his own time and in his own way.

It is summed up beautifully in Psalm 46:10 (NRSV). 'Be still and know that I am God!' The meaning of 'be still' in this verse is literally 'let go'. Let go, in the sure knowledge that God himself will act, like relaxing into free fall, in the confident certainty that the parachute will open at the crucial moment!

# Letting go of judgement

At the beginning of John chapter 8, a heart-rending story is recounted of a woman caught in the act of adultery and dragged in by the religious leaders of the day to stand trial before Jesus. As far as the self-righteous Pharisees were concerned, their only agenda was accusation and judgement. They were revelling in the dual opportunity to humiliate the woman and compromise Jesus. But Jesus placed the ball back squarely where it belonged – in their court, by challenging them to examine their own lives, not someone else's. This challenge is echoed in Romans 14:4 (NIV): 'Who are you to judge someone else's servant? To his own master he stands or falls.'

When the last of the Pharisees had finally slunk

away, the woman was left face to face with her master only, and that alone was the appropriate context for dialogue to begin about her sin.

God has had to impress this on my heart in my attitude to James. I have no responsibility or remit to judge. All of *my* responsibility is encompassed in 1 Peter 4:7 (J.B. Phillips) – 'You should therefore be calm, self-controlled men (women) of prayer. Above everything else, be sure that you have real, deep love for each other, remembering how love can cover a multitude of sins.'

'Grey' areas – sin – are inherent in all relationships, mine as well as my children's, but God alone has the remit for sorting this out. My responsibility, I realised, was the 'deep love that covers'; the love that holds the door open for access to a tender, compassionate God; the love that never provokes a hindrance or a stumbling-block to God's patient dealings with his own.

Romans 14:4 (NIV) ends with a triumphant assertion: 'And he will stand, for God is able to make him stand.' We can ask nothing more for our children.

**Step two**

# Letting go of self-reproach

Much has been written and debated about the 'causes' of homosexuality and a common theory is that the blame lies with an over-possessive, dominant mother. As the mother of a homosexual son (and, again, I'm sure I'm not alone in my self-reproach) I have therefore done my share of agonising over whether I'm 'to blame'.

Certainly, I have always had a very close relationship with my middle son, but then we are very alike in personality, very much on the same wavelength. I don't think I have been guilty of over-possessiveness or a domineering attitude, but at the same time I'm sure I have made my fair share of mistakes in James's upbringing, just as I have with my other two children.

Ultimately I have had to accept that agonising over my possible past deficiencies as a mother is pointless and destructive. Psalm 139 (AV) refers specifically to covering us in our mother's womb. 'Covering', with its connotations of shelter and protection, means that, right from embryo stage, God is sovereign in the care of his child.

The story of Isaac's birth and upbringing in Genesis was chequered with parental unbelief and maternal possessiveness. His very name signifies laughter, not only the positive laughter of pure joy in the birth of a son granted to long-barren parents, but the incredulous laughter of mocking disbelief in the face of a promise from God.

But the very ambiguity of his name is a great source of encouragement to me. The name was an inescapable reminder throughout Isaac's life of parental mistakes and unbelief, but it was also an earnest of God's plan and purpose in the young man's life. These two strands, running through the one ambiguous name, were indivisible.

I also found another kind of ambiguity, along the same kind of lines, in Galatians 1:15 (NRSV) – 'But when God, who had set me apart before I was born ...'

I believe that God has been carrying out his special commissioning and setting apart work in the lives of all my children, from before they were born, regardless of the fallibility of their human parents. For James, though, perhaps this setting apart involves something else as well – a true 'setting apart' in terms of belonging to a sadly persecuted minority group.

We would never choose such a membership for our children, but God is in the business of seeking outcasts. Mercifully, his agenda is quite different from that element of the church that bears his name but continues to ostracise and demonise gay people. As long as this tragic state of affairs exists, I believe that God will create individuals to be part of a group whose hunger for the knowledge of his all-embracing love is often cruelly denied.

So I thank God for all the faithful gay Christians of whom God says, 'They are my servants ... in whom I will be glorified' (Isaiah 49:3 NRSV). They alone are equipped for the Christlike ministry of entering into the special experience of a minority group.

# Letting go of anxiety

From time to time, I find myself fretting about the future quality of James's life, how his human needs will be fulfilled for love, companionship, a home, family life. Psalm 91 (NIV) has been a great means of encouragement to me over many of these anxieties, particularly the last verse of that psalm. 'With long life will I satisfy him (or as the Living Bible says, 'with a *full* life'), and show him my salvation' (v16).

'A full life', I realised, may be based on a wide variety of criteria, and not just the ones I had envisaged for each of my sons. God had to convince me that 'his ways' aren't necessarily 'my ways' on this (Isaiah 55:8 NRSV), that when he pledges 'life in all its fullness' (John 10:10 LB), the promise applies to every believer, but not according to the same, identical 'happiness blueprint'.

James has a great gift for friendship. His phone bill testifies to a rich network of friendships all over the world! My fears that he will ever live a lonely, loveless life are probably groundless.

But, most importantly, I have to trust God for '*his* salvation' in each of my children's lives – broad, exciting, creative, uniquely fitted to each of them as people. Abundant life is a certainty; its specific outworking, I have to realise, is God's highly individual enterprise.

# Letting go of dreams

When Abraham received the promise of the birth of Isaac, God said, 'I will establish my covenant *with him* for an everlasting covenant.' Even pre-birth, God was talking in terms of a covenant relationship with Isaac that already precluded Abraham or Sarah.

So years later, when Abraham was making that terrible pilgrimage up Mount Moriah, the young man Isaac at his side, laden with the wood for his own sacrifice, Abraham must surely have taken refuge in the memory of that covenant promise. As far as he could see, the climb up Mount Moriah signified a cruel end to all his treasured hopes and dreams for the lad, but scraping rock bottom of his own resources and understanding in the situation, he came up with a poignant expression of faith. 'My son,

God will provide himself a lamb ...' (Genesis 22:8 AV).

God had made a personal covenant with Isaac, and Abraham must have had all sorts of preconceived ideas about how this would work out. Like any proud parent, he would have indulged in daydreams about his offspring's glittering future, but on Mount Moriah he had to hand the dreams over to God. When, against all human odds, he acknowledged that God would provide, he was accepting that God's ways were higher than his, that all he could do in the situation was be available – available to listen to God and available to walk, step by step, up that terrible mountain track with his son.

Probably Abraham didn't realise it at the time, but God, in his faithfulness, was exchanging his empty daydreams for something far more precious. Abraham's relationship with both God and his son must have been transformed and deepened for ever that perplexing day on Mount Moriah.

Perhaps it's only at the point where we sacrifice our own superficial dreams for our children that God can do the same for us.

## Step five

# Letting go of authority

The Gospels contain several accounts of Jesus raising the dead, and the brief account in Luke 7:11–15 (NIV) of his restoring the widow of Nain's son is one of the most touching.

He encountered the pathetic funeral procession as it made its way out of the city. 'As he approached the town gate, a dead person was being carried out – the only son of his mother, and she was a widow.'

There was a sense in which, when James first told me he was homosexual, I had to cope with grief that felt like bereavement, as though a person I had known was gone and I was faced with getting acquainted with a stranger. I also grieved for the loss of future grandchildren.

Happily, this grief-stricken reaction passed very quickly but the account of 'a dead person being carried out' seemed layered with meaning for me. All our perceptions of others, even those we know and love most deeply, are distorted by our own preconceptions, our own illusions about them, and sometimes these illusions have to be put to death and 'carried out', in order for our relationships to deepen and mature.

This mother was grieving over a dead person and Jesus's 'heart went out to her' but she had to stand aside in this situation and allow the vital transaction to be between Jesus and her son. At the Lord's touch on the coffin, even the coffin-bearers had to stand still. 'Stand still and see the salvation of the Lord' (Exodus 14:13 AV).

The injunction to 'stand still' can be a blessedly liberating one. I don't have all or perhaps any of the answers regarding the issue of homosexuality. As a heterosexual, there is much that I find impossible to understand about a different kind of sexuality, but Jesus has entered into every experience and feeling known to humankind. He alone is qualified to deal with homosexual Christians on how to live their lives.

The widow of Nain was faced with the equally perplexing fact of death. Her son had entered into an experience that she couldn't share and was powerless to reverse. She had no choice but to stand still and let Christ deal with it.

Ultimately, she was to experience the joy of having her son restored to her, but the dialogue of this miracle was an intensely personal one: 'Young man, *I say unto thee*, Arise.'

Perhaps this widowed mother wasn't used to being excluded, perhaps dependence on an only son had become possessiveness. We can only conjecture. But the son she received back from the dead was on Jesus's terms, not hers and, from that day on and for all eternity, the divine authority, the ringing words of the Master's 'Arise', would have superseded all other authority in that young man's life.

Three

# The Journey Inward

One thing that I began to realise fairly early on in this specific spiritual journey God had organised for me was that the experience of working through my attitude as regards James was revealing deep areas of need in my own life.

Psalm 115:14–15 (NIV) says: 'May the Lord make you increase, *both you and your children.*' In my initial absorption with James's needs, it was easy for me to overlook that God had a lot of transforming to do in my own life as I dealt with this experience.

I remembered with shame, many years earlier, when my children were only toddlers, how harsh I had been in my private verbal judgement of a young curate at our church whose homosexuality had been revealed through an incident that resulted in a court case. As far as I was concerned, his particular temptations were alien to me and I made no attempt to understand or to show compassion.

I would have been horrified then to term this reaction by such an ugly name as homophobia, but God knew what it was, and in his own time he knew it had to be tackled and rooted out. His patient commitment to dealing with this in my life was entirely consistent with James 1:4 (AV) – 'But let patience have her perfect work, that ye may be perfect and entire, *lacking nothing.*'

At the beginning of the book of Ruth, faced with bereavement and loss, Ruth's mother-in-law Naomi says: 'I went away full but the Lord has brought me back empty.' (Ruth 1:21 NIV) At that point, she was experiencing only the emptiness; she had no intuition of all that God had in store, the new things he was preparing to fill her emptiness, so that she might 'lack nothing'.

The 'rooting out' process is a painful, 'emptying' one, but God was also beginning to impress on me that it is also a preparation for the 'increase' he plans for my life and for the lives of all those I love.

## Step one

# 'Coming out of the cave'

*When my spirit was overwhelmed within me, then thou knewest my path.*
(Ps 142:3 AV)

David wrote these words from the gloomy depths of a cave that he'd taken refuge in when he was being pursued by his enemies. He was overwhelmed; he didn't know how to cope, but he clung on to one fact, that God knew his path, that God had planned his journey.

I was reminded of David and his cave one day when reading John 11 (AV) and the account of the raising of Lazarus. My attention was drawn particularly to Mary,

Lazarus's sister. She and her sister Martha had sent a message to Jesus when their brother fell gravely ill, a simple statement of faith and helplessness: 'Lord, behold, he whom thou lovest is sick.' All they could do was point to the need in their beloved brother's life and rely on the fact that Jesus loved him. A beautiful 'handing over responsibility' prayer if ever there was one!

But its answer took a while coming and in that time Mary retreated into her own cave of hurt and resentment. When Jesus arrived at her home village two days later – too late it seemed, for her brother had since died – she stayed where she was in the house. When she finally responded to Jesus's request to see her, her first bitter words to her Master were heavy with hurt and reproach: 'Lord if thou hadst been here, my brother had not died.'

Even though he knew she was about to witness a far greater miracle than mere healing, Jesus refrained from any rebuke about her lack of faith. Instead, he simply wept with her. He sat down for a while next to her in her 'cave' and simply entered into how she felt.

In the early days of just trying to take in the fact of James's homosexuality, that was precisely what I needed. I needed to be able to sob out all my hurt and fears and resentments to God. I needed to be honest about all the questions I had. I needed to express anger to him, to tell him that I didn't see at all how this fitted in with his love and faithfulness. In short, I needed to experience the truth of Psalm 34:18 (NRSV) – 'The Lord is near to the brokenhearted.'

God, I discovered, doesn't hurry or bypass this process because the deepest miracle is here. Even a mighty act like raising the dead is dwarfed by the miracle that takes place in the human heart through learning to trust him without necessarily seeing the answers; to affirm our love for him when his dealings are inexplicable. Mary had to be called out of her 'cave' of despondency and despair before Lazarus could be called out of his.

## Step two

# 'No superficial cure'

Like many Christians, I have been guilty in the past of viewing homosexuality as some kind of deep-seated sickness that requires healing. The end result of this kind of thinking is to subject homosexual Christians to a relentless prayer regime aimed at turning them into heterosexuals, since the healing of such a condition is the only alternative to modern-day excommunication.

James himself has listened to testimonies from homosexual Christians who claim to have been healed, and one of the questions it raises for him is whether these 'healed' homosexuals will ever feel any future compassion for the homosexual community, any compunction to identify with their spiritual needs and point the way to Christ.

Having shaken the 'homosexual' dust from their feet, I'm sure the answer is 'No', in which case, their supposed healing is surely a very superficial cure.

This was borne in on me one day, almost as a sequel to the raising Lazarus account, when I read about what was probably Mary of Bethany's last human encounter with Christ. In Matthew 27:55 (NRSV) we are told that, at Jesus's crucifixion, 'many women were also there, looking on from a distance'.

If Mary was among these women, as seems likely, I'm sure she would have had vivid memories of the day that Jesus had raised her brother from the dead. Now she had to watch this same Jesus submitting himself to death, when he, above all others, could surely have saved himself.

But perhaps she had some inkling that day, at the foot of a terrible bloodied cross, that she was seeing a deeper solution being worked out, that Lazarus's resurrection had only been a temporary one which hadn't begun to deal with the fundamental fact of death. The raising of her beloved brother had been the solution that Mary craved and received, but at the cross she would have been aware that another woman stood nearby for whom the solution wasn't going to be that instant or that simple. Mary, the mother of Jesus, had to experience the pain of seeing her son submit himself to death so that the final solution could be real and eternal.

# The challenge to self-centredness

'After these things, the word of the Lord came unto Abram in a vision saying, Fear not Abram: I am thy shield and thy exceedingly great reward. And Abram said, Lord God, what wilt thou give me, seeing I go childless?'

When I came across these verses recently, at the beginning of Genesis 15 (AV), I identified particularly with Abraham's artless, rather childlike prayer, 'What wilt thou give me?' I identified with it because its utter self-centredness was so similar to many of my own attitudes. His vision, in terms of fathering offspring, extended only as far as how the birth of a child would gratify *him*. His prayer contained no sense of how God's purposes might be accomplished through that child.

Similarly, Sarah's reaction at the birth of Isaac is tellingly centred on the word 'me'. 'God has brought me laughter, and everyone who hears about this will laugh with me' (Genesis 21:6 NIV). Her joy is touching, but perhaps the seeds of self-centred possessiveness were sown there and bore bitter fruit when she ruthlessly banished Hagar, along with her son Ishmael, from her household – 'For the son of this bond woman shall not be heir with *my* son.' There's no sense of compassion here, no hint of compunction that another mother, with an equally cherished son, was being hounded out so that they could both perish in the wilderness.

As a parent, I'm not alone in the desire to see dreams and aspirations realised through my children. Similarly, every parent wants to protect their child from harmful, negative influence. But in striving to accept that my middle son was homosexual, I had to face up to the reality that part of my inner struggle was based on the fact that homosexuality didn't fit with my own ideas and aspirations for him. My reaction had nothing to do with believing in God's purpose for his life.

The recent 'Keep the Clause' debacle in Scotland featured many Christian mothers campaigning to protect their children, and the family in general, from the 'taint' of homosexuality, claiming that any discussion of homosexuality in classrooms was symptomatic of godless moral decline. How many of these mothers may yet discover that one of their own children is gay? I can only pray that such a revelation would engender a new spirit of compassion for all the banished 'Ishmaels', the ones who have been hounded out of school playgrounds, taunted with the slogan 'Keep the Clause'.

Abraham was given a new spirit, as his words to his servants on Mount Moriah testify. When the time came for the final, awesome ascent to the sacrifice, he was utterly focused on God and had committed his own life and his son's unreservedly into God's hands. 'I and the lad will go yonder and *worship*' (Genesis 22:5 AV).

**Step four**

# Coming to terms with the 'cannots'

Like all mothers, I have a deep, instinctive desire to protect my children. A great deal of my concern for James, therefore, is bound up with anxiety about what he may have to suffer as a homosexual, the problems he might face from being 'different'.

In Matthew 6:27 (NIV), Jesus refers to this kind of pointless anxiety when he asks, 'Who of you by worrying can add a single hour to his life?' I realised as I read this that I too was agonising over something I was powerless to change.

Then I went on to read Psalm 22:29 (NIV) and was brought up short by a single phrase there: 'those who cannot keep themselves alive'. Every day of my life, I have to trust God with the most fundamental 'cannot' of all, the impossibility of keeping my own heart beating. Already God does for me, every minute of the day, what I cannot do for myself – he keeps me alive. Surely, then, I can trust him with my other 'cannots', the other places where I am utterly powerless.

Last Easter, at a Good Friday service at our church, we were led in a meditation on one of Christ's utterances from the cross, 'My God, my God, why hast thou forsaken me?' Still thinking about my own powerlessness, I was awed and deeply moved by the thought that God, the Father, rendered himself powerless to act on behalf of his own son, during those long, terrible hours that he hung on the cross. In order for Christ to fulfil the purpose for which he came into the world, his Heavenly Father had to abrogate power and make himself helpless to intervene. He had to watch his beloved child go through the most intense and complete pain there has ever been in the world and to embrace powerlessness to allow him to do it.

I was humbled and greatly comforted to realise that God had even shared the experience of my 'cannots', that the heartache of having to stand back and allow the possibility of pain in my child's life was yet another example of an experience in which God had already gone before.

# The call to joy

Psalm 113:9 (AV) says: 'He maketh the barren woman to keep house and to be a joyful mother of children.'

Years ago, as the harassed mother of toddlers, I used to read that verse ruefully from time to time, praying that I wouldn't just manage to make it through the day until my children's bedtime, but that I'd do it with joy!

Now, almost a couple of decades later, I was faced with the same challenge. Was I just going to 'make it through' in my attitude to my middle son, or was I going to embrace his situation and the person he is with joy?

In Acts 27, the apostle Paul gives us a graphic account of a terrible storm at sea, a ship's crew and passengers in fear of their lives. Yet above the crash of the waves, Paul's voice rings out with amazing confidence urging them to be positive. 'And now I exhort you to be of good cheer,' he says, 'for there shall be no loss of any man's life among you … and lo, God hath given thee all them that sail with thee. Wherefore sirs, be of good cheer; for I believe God that it shall be even as it was told me' (Acts 27:22–25 AV).

Life brings its squalls and its storms and I'd be lying if I tried to pretend that struggling to come to terms with James's homosexuality didn't number among one of my most overwhelming storms to date. But I believe God when he says that there will be no loss, no waste of his life as a result, and that when God promises to give me all the precious people that 'sail' with me, all really does mean all.

# Four

# The Journey 'Outside the Gate'

*Wherefore Jesus also, that he might sanctify the people with his own blood, suffered outside the gate. Let us go forth, therefore, unto Him outside the camp, bearing his reproach.*
(Heb. 13:12,13 AV)

Bound up with our ambitions for our children is usually the desire that they should be popular, accepted by their peers, secure in their place in society. But intrinsic in being homosexual is the fact of belonging to a minority group, of being spurned by some sectors of society, the butt of crass, insensitive jokes, the victims of a great deal of ignorant prejudice.

Yet the heartache of being an outsider is one that Christ knew intimately and if his call to my child is to join him 'outside the gate', then the challenge to me is surely to trust him with all that is involved in that call.

Genesis 22:6 (NRSV) records: 'Abraham took the wood of the burnt offering and laid it on his son Isaac.'

Incapable of shouldering the burden himself, how cruel and poignant it must have seemed to Abraham to see his son's back bent under the weight of the wood for his own sacrifice. Yet it occurred to me as I thought about this passage that from another perspective it represented a beautiful foreshadowing of the path God's own Son would take, bearing the weight of his wooden cross to Calvary.

We may bitterly regret the burdens our children have to shoulder, and this applies whatever their sexual orientation, but we also have the choice over which perspective to take.

In closing, I think I can express this thought best in a poem I wrote during a retreat I took part in last year, as I meditated on the verses already mentioned, in Genesis 22, that deal with Abraham's journey to sacrifice Isaac. The words don't represent great poetry, but they encapsulate something for me that I feel I'd like to pass on.

## Climbing Mount Moriah

I cursed the cruel burden
on a back so young and strong
I questioned how a loving God
could commit so great a wrong

I wept at my own frail helplessness
to alleviate the load
I gazed at my son with heavy heart
trudging next to me on the road.

I could not bear to see the strain
that twisted his young face
I would have given anything
to somehow take his place

But as I turned to look ahead
my vision blurred with tears
I saw another figure
who alone could quiet my fears

His back was bent just like my son's
as he turned his feet to go
beyond the city walls
to a place that only outsiders know

You cannot take him there my Lord
the journey is too great
He'll faint before it's ended
bearing such a desperate weight.

The figure only smiled at me
hand outstretched to my son,
I saw them take their way in step
as though the two were one.

And I knew my bitter questions
had been silenced by my God
who only planned to take my child
the way His feet had trod.

And I thought of another Parent
a trembling hand, a brimming cup
and a voice that gently urged me, 'Take,
and gladly drink it up.'

My journey continues. But like Mary in the garden on the first Easter morning, I'm learning that many of my fears have been based on the anguished cry, 'I know not' (John 20:13 AV).

Her weeping, like mine, stemmed from the heartache of what she didn't understand and her tears prevented her, initially, from seeing Jesus, present with her in the midst of what she interpreted as a desolate situation.

In the Old Testament account of Jacob's journey (Genesis 28:16 AV) we are told that Jacob woke from his prophetic dream with these words on his lips: 'Surely the Lord is in this place and I knew it not.'

May this also be true for your journey, just as it is for mine.

# Biblical sources

AV: King James Authorised Version, Oxford University Press, 1967.

J.B. Phillips: New Testament in Modern English, published by Geoffrey Bles Ltd, 1968.

LB: The Living Bible copyright © Tyndale House Publishers 1971.

NIV: New International Version, copyright © 1973, 1978, 1984 International Bible Society. Hodder & Stoughton 1980 edition.

NRSV: New Revised Standard Version, copyright © 1989 Division of Christian Education of the National Council of the Churches of Christ in the USA. Printed in Great Britain at the University Press, Cambridge.

# Also from Wild Goose Publications...

## Praying with Our Hands

*21 practices of embodied prayer from the world's spiritual traditions*

Jon Sweeney

A book of reflections and accompanying photographs showing simple ways of using our hands and bodies to speak to God. These spiritual practices are drawn from a broad range of religious traditions – from Anglican to Sufi, from Buddhist to Shaker. Some may be familiar; some new; all demonstrate the universal importance people of all faith traditions have given to embodied prayer.

96pp · 1 901557 59 6 · £10.99

## The One Loaf

*An everyday celebration*

Joy Mead

An illustrated book of stories, recipes, poems and prayers which explores the making and the mystery of bread – its growing, making and baking, and the holiness of eating and the justice of sharing.

160pp · 1 901557 38 3 · £10.99

## Lent & Easter Readings from Iona

Neil Paynter (ed)

A book of readings from members and staff of the Iona Community which aims to help us reappraise our lives during the period leading up to Easter.

160pp · 1 901557 62 6 · £8.99

## The Iona Abbey Worship Book

### The Iona Community

Services and resources used daily in the Abbey on the island of Iona reflecting the Iona Community's commitment to the belief that worship is all that we are and all that we do, with no division into the 'sacred' and the 'secular'. The material draws on many traditions, including the Celtic.

272pp · 1 901557 50 2 · £9.99

## Praying for the Dawn

*A resource book for the ministry of healing*

### Ruth Burgess and Kathy Galloway (eds)

A compilation of material from several writers with a strong emphasis on liturgies and resources for healing services. Many aspects of healing are addressed and the book includes a section of worship resources – prayers, responses, litanies, poems, meditations and blessings.

192pp · 1 901557 26 X · £10.99

## My Dinner With Anton

*A book about St Seraphim of Sarov*

### Paul Wallis

An extraordinary over-dinner conversation between a 19th-century Russian Orthodox monk and a contemporary minister about the life and example of an intriguing Russian saint, Seraphim of Sarov, and the relevance of his teaching to modern western spirituality.

128pp · 1 901557 31 6 · £8.99

# The Iona Community

The Iona Community, founded in 1938 by the Revd George MacLeod, then a parish minister in Glasgow, is an ecumenical Christian community committed to seeking new ways of living the Gospel in today's world. Initially working to restore part of the medieval abbey on Iona, the Community today remains committed to 'rebuilding the common life' through working for social and political change, striving for the renewal of the church with an ecumenical emphasis, and exploring new, more inclusive approaches to worship, all based on an integrated understanding of spirituality.

The Community now has over 240 Members, about 1500 Associate Members and around 1500 Friends. The Members – women and men from many denominations and backgrounds (lay and ordained), living throughout Britain with a few overseas – are committed to a fivefold Rule of devotional discipline, sharing and accounting for use of time and money, regular meeting, and action for justice and peace.

At the Community's three residential centres – the Abbey and the MacLeod Centre on Iona, and Camas Adventure Camp on the Ross of Mull – guests are welcomed from March to October and over Christmas. Hospitality is provided for over 110 people, along with a unique opportunity, usually through week-long programmes, to extend horizons and forge relationships through sharing an experience of the common life in worship, work, discussion and relaxation. The Community's shop on Iona, just outside the Abbey grounds, carries an attractive range of books and craft goods.

The Community's administrative headquarters are in Glasgow, which also serves as a base for its work with young people, the Wild Goose Resource Group working in the field of worship, a bi-monthly magazine, *Coracle*, and a publishing house, Wild Goose Publications.

*For information on the Iona Community contact:*
The Iona Community
Fourth Floor, Savoy House, 140 Sauchiehall Street,
Glasgow G2 3DH, UK
Phone: +44 (0)141 332 6343
e-mail: ionacomm@gla.iona.org.uk    web: www.iona.org.uk

*For enquiries about visiting Iona, please contact:*
Iona Abbey
Isle of Iona
Argyll PA76 6SN, UK
Phone: +44 (0)1681 700404    e-mail: ionacomm@iona.org.uk

*For book/tape/CD catalogues, contact:*
Wild Goose Publications
Fourth Floor, Savoy House, 140 Sauchiehall Street,
Glasgow G2 3DH, UK
Tel. +44 (0)141 332 6292
Fax +44 (0)141 332 1090
e-mail: admin@ionabooks.com
or see and purchase our products online at
www.ionabooks.com